Original title:
Snowlace

Copyright © 2024 Swan Charm
All rights reserved.

Author: Swan Charm
ISBN HARDBACK: 978-9916-79-747-1
ISBN PAPERBACK: 978-9916-79-748-8
ISBN EBOOK: 978-9916-79-749-5

Artistry of Nature's Frosted Palette

In the hush of winter's breath,
Whispers of white coats the ground,
Branches draped in silken threads,
A quiet magic all around.

Glistening gems on the pond's face,
Each crystal catches morning light,
Nature paints with delicate grace,
Transforming dark to purest white.

Footprints etched in sparkling snow,
A symphony of silence plays,
Frosted leaves in a gentle glow,
Sculpting beauty through the days.

Underneath the midnight sky,
Stars twinkle like frost-kissed trees,
Winter wraps the world with sighs,
In its grandeur, hearts find ease.

As the dawn breaks, hues unfold,
Pastels dance in soft embrace,
Nature's art, a story told,
In every flake, a wild grace.

Winter's Tapestry

The frost weaves tales of light,
Whispers float on the wind's sigh.
Each flake a note in the night,
As the soft stars drift by.

Trees wear coats of crystal white,
Blankets hug the sleeping ground.
Moonlight dances with delight,
In this beauty, peace is found.

Footprints trace a silent path,
Echoes of laughter in the cold.
Nature's art calls for a laugh,
In a world of silver and gold.

As shadows stretch and fade away,
Time feels still in the night's embrace.
Dreams unfold in soft array,
Winter's charm a warm embrace.

Underneath the starry dome,
Hearts gather, stories unfold.
In this season, we find home,
In its beauty, our lives told.

Enchanted Snowfall

Snowflakes dance through moonlit skies,
As the earth dons a cloak so fair.
Time pauses, and beauty lies,
In each crystal, love and care.

Whispers of winter fill the air,
Crisp and cool like a gentle song.
Magic lingers everywhere,
In this enchantment, we belong.

The world covered in shimmering white,
Every branch glistens with delight.
A hush falls softly throughout the night,
In the glow of the moon's soft light.

Hearts awaken in this spell,
Beneath the blanket, dreams ignite.
In this wonder, all is well,
Lost in the warmth of pure delight.

Each moment, a treasure we keep,
As the snow falls in peaceful calm.
In the stillness, our spirits leap,
Finding solace in nature's balm.

A Glint of Serenity

Amidst the blizzard's swirling dance,
A moment's peace takes gentle form.
In the quiet, we find our chance,
To calm the chaos, find the warm.

The world glows with a silver sheen,
Nature whispers secrets untold.
In this hush, life feels serene,
As winter's magic begins to unfold.

Birds rest on branches, still and bright,
Stars twinkle in the deep blue night.
In this calm, we hold on tight,
Finding comfort in soft starlight.

Footprints tracing paths of dreams,
In the blanket of the snowy ground.
Among the stillness, hope redeems,
A glint of peace in silence found.

As dawn breaks in a soft embrace,
The world awakens, fresh and free.
In winter's arms, we find our place,
A glint of joy, our hearts agree.

Chilling Reverie

The wind whispers tales of old,
As it weaves through trees so bare.
In the chill, stories unfold,
A reverie in the frosty air.

Icicles hang like jewels bright,
Glimmering in the day's soft glow.
Every breath a cloud of white,
In this beauty, time seems slow.

Frosted windows frame the scene,
Where warmth lingers, and love calls.
In this magic, we can glean,
The wonder that winter enthralls.

A calming hush wraps us tight,
While outside, the world is bold.
In this quiet, hearts take flight,
In the chilling embrace we hold.

As twilight paints the sky anew,
Our dreams drift like snowflakes down.
In this moment, together we view,
A reverie's peace, winter's crown.

Slumbering Hues of Icy Grace

In twilight's soft embrace, they lie,
A world adorned, beneath the sky.
Shades of blue and silver blend,
As day and night in whispers end.

Frozen secrets, nature's art,
In quiet realms, they play their part.
Each shadow dances, dreams take flight,
In the arms of tender night.

Crystal rivers, silent streams,
Hold the whispers of our dreams.
Together bound in time's embrace,
We drift within, this icy grace.

Glacial Veils in a Stillness Lullaby

Beneath the stars, a stillness grows,
Wrapped in veils of ice and prose.
A lullaby of frost it sings,
While moonlight weaves its silken strings.

In breathless nights, the silence sighs,
As winter's touch draws gentle skies.
Every flake, a tale untold,
A moment trapped, a spark of gold.

Glistening whispers fill the air,
Soft as secrets, light as prayer.
Each heartbeat echoes winter's song,
A splendor vast and deep, yet strong.

Pearl-like Embers of the Frost

In the hush of wintry days,
Glimmers rise in soft arrays.
Pearl-like embers gently gleam,
Whispering of a frozen dream.

Shimmering on the night's cool breath,
Echoes of a silent death.
Yet in that pause, life softly stirs,
As nature's pulse still gently whirs.

Each moment held, suspended, bright,
In frost's embrace, a dance of light.
A fleeting glimpse, this magic breath,
In beauty's gaze, we conquer death.

Intricate Lace of the Winter's Hand

The winter's hand weaves lace so fine,
A tapestry of frost and shine.
Patterns dance on window panes,
In elegant forms, silence reigns.

Beneath the snow, the earth does dream,
In quiet hues, a gentle theme.
Each flake a note in nature's score,
An artful magic, forevermore.

Time glides softly, as shadows play,
On intricate paths where we stray.
In every thread, a story spins,
Of winter's love where our tale begins.

Frosted Whimsy

In the quiet of night so bright,
Frosted whispers take their flight.
Dancing lightly on the trees,
Nature breathes with gentle ease.

Twinkling stars like diamonds glow,
Painting dreams on earth below.
Each step soft upon the ground,
Magic lingers all around.

Branches wear a crystal gown,
While shimmers gently touch the town.
A world wrapped in winter's lace,
Time slows down in this pure space.

Breezes hum a lullaby,
To the moon that drifts so high.
Frosted whimsy fills the air,
Enchanting hearts beyond compare.

Celestial Crystals

Beyond the clouds where shadows hide,
Celestial crystals do abide.
Glimmers from a distant sphere,
Calling out for hearts to cheer.

Stars like droplets softly fall,
Whispers floating, nature's call.
In the silence, dreams ignite,
Guided by the velvet night.

Lights of silver, pure and sweet,
Kissing softly every street.
Through the dark, a path unfolds,
With secrets waiting to be told.

Infinite as time may be,
A tapestry of destiny.
Celestial dance, a cosmic play,
Embracing hope in every ray.

The Frost that Binds

Winter's breath, so crisp and clear,
Weaves a tale that draws us near.
Threads of frost like silver twine,
Binding hearts with love divine.

In the stillness, whispers freeze,
Nature's palette, rich as trees.
Every flake a story spun,
In the glow of setting sun.

Footprints soft in powder white,
Mark the dreams that take their flight.
Underneath the icy sheen,
Lives the hope of springtime green.

Together in the frozen scene,
Shadows dance, and visions gleam.
The frost that binds, a gentle tether,
Drawing souls to come together.

Layered Serenity

Gentle layers softly blend,
Whispers of the world transcend.
Each snowfall, a calming breath,
Cradling life, a dance with death.

Silence wraps the earth in peace,
In this stillness, thoughts release.
A canvas pure, untouched by time,
Layered serenity, so sublime.

Nature's brush paints winter's song,
In the quiet, hearts belong.
Harmony in every flake,
A sacred stillness we partake.

Finding solace in the chill,
Moments shared, hearts gently fill.
Layered serenity we find,
In the whispers, love defined.

The Winter Weaving of Time

In the hush of snowflakes falling,
Threads of silence weave the day.
Time stands still, softly calling,
As winter's magic comes to play.

Frosted branches whisper secrets,
Nature's quilt, so pure and bright.
Each step leaves a tale, it begets,
In the glow of the silver light.

The chilling breath of distant dawn,
Weaves the past with threads of white.
Winter's hands, they gently fawn,
Over dreams that dance in night.

Days grow short, yet stars ignite,
In skies that hold the winter's grace.
Through the tapestry of night,
Time is stitched in soft embrace.

So gather 'round, let stories flow,
In this season's tender rhyme.
As we wander through the snow,
In the winter weaving of time.

Subtle Stories of Winter's Touch

Quiet whispers fill the air,
As winter weaves its gentle art.
Each breath a story, a moment rare,
In the cold, we find the heart.

Branches cloaked in crystal sheen,
Dance with shadows, light and dark.
Every flake a silver dream,
Painting worlds with a sparkling mark.

Beneath the stars, soft snow descends,
Wrapping earth in a tender sigh.
Nature breathes, the quiet bends,
As dreams drift under the frosty sky.

In every corner, tales unfold,
Of silent nights and glimmering days.
Winter whispers, subtle and bold,
In the melody of its frosted ways.

So let us gather, warm and near,
In the stories spun of snow's embrace.
For in winter's touch, nothing to fear,
Just subtle secrets, time leaves no trace.

A Dream in Frosted Hues

In the stillness of the night,
Frosted dreams begin to bloom.
Colors swirl in soft delight,
Painting shadows, chasing gloom.

Whispers float on icy breath,
Through twilight's gentle sighs we glide.
Each moment holds the kiss of death,
And life anew, where dreams abide.

Windows glisten, tales unfold,
In every breath, a wish is made.
Winter's magic, bright and bold,
In a tapestry of light and shade.

Stars emerge from velvet skies,
Crystals dance upon the ground.
In the silence, hope will rise,
Amidst the beauty all around.

So close your eyes, let dreams pursue,
In the night where wishes blend.
A world alive in frosted hues,
Where time and magic softly mend.

Glacial Secrets in Nature's Embrace

Amidst the ice, a story sleeps,
Veiled in silence, deep and true.
Nature holds what gently keeps,
Secrets old and wisdom new.

Beneath the surface, life awaits,
In shards of blue and white so bright.
Echoes dance at winter's gates,
Fingers tracing in the night.

The glacial breath, it tells of time,
Of ages past and futures clear.
Nature's song, a timeless rhyme,
In whispers only few can hear.

Cascading down from frosty heights,
The world transforms in frozen grace.
With every drift, with all its sights,
Glacial secrets softly trace.

So let us wander, hearts ablaze,
In nature's chill, we find our place.
For in the snow's embracing gaze,
Lie glacial secrets, wrapped in grace.

Whispers of Winter

Gentle breezes sweep the land,
Snowflakes twirl, a soft white band.
Silent nights and frosty air,
Nature wraps us, calm and rare.

Footprints left in purest white,
Echoes of the day take flight.
In the stillness, secrets roam,
Winter's hush, a whispered home.

Beneath the boughs where shadows creep,
Dreams of warmth and fires we keep.
Fireside tales of days gone by,
As the snowflakes gently sigh.

Stars above, like diamonds shine,
In winter's grip, our hearts entwine.
The world dressed in silver glow,
Whispers of winter softly flow.

Frosted Dreams

In the morn, a world aglow,
Frosted dreams in shimmering show.
Nature's canvas, pure and bright,
Every crystal catches light.

Icicles hang like precious jewels,
Beauty formed by nature's rules.
Underneath the icy sheen,
Winter whispers, calm and keen.

Snow-capped hills invite our gaze,
Silent hearts in winter's haze.
Sleds and laughter fill the air,
Joyful moments everywhere.

From frosty breath to glistening trees,
Each sight invites a gentle breeze.
In this realm where dreams take flight,
Frosted dreams bring pure delight.

Crystal Embrace

With every breath, the cold does cling,
Nature wrapped in winter's ring.
Frosted branches, a crystal lace,
In the heart, a warm embrace.

Snowflakes fall, a gentle dance,
Caught in whispers, lost in trance.
Each one unique, a work of art,
In winter's glow, they melt the heart.

As twilight casts its dreamy hue,
The world transforms, a crystal view.
In this silence, peace does bloom,
Winter's gift dispels the gloom.

In shimmering fields, we find our way,
Through the hush of another day.
With hope and dreams that never cease,
In winter's arms, we find our peace.

The Dance of Winter's Veil

In the stillness, shadows sway,
Winter's dance begins to play.
Snowflakes twirl like dancers' feet,
Nature's rhythm, soft and sweet.

Every breath a cloud of white,
Day fades gently into night.
Fireside warmth, a cozy nest,
As winter whispers, we find rest.

Glistening paths beneath the moon,
Echoes of a frosty tune.
With every step, the world unfolds,
Stories whispered, yet untold.

In winter's grasp, we come alive,
With hope, heart, and dreams to thrive.
The dance of winter, a sweet embrace,
In every flake, a loving trace.

Frost's Tender Caress

In the hush of dawn's first light,
Frost glimmers, pure and bright.
Each blade of grass, a crystal knife,
Chasing dreams, embracing life.

Whispers dance on chilly air,
A gentle touch beyond compare.
Nature's breath, a frosty sigh,
Promises borne, as night winds fly.

Patterns woven, subtle grace,
Time stands still in this soft space.
A moment held, a quiet thrill,
Frost's embrace forever still.

Underneath the glowing moon,
Silent world, a wistful tune.
In the night, each glitter beams,
Awakens all our hidden dreams.

In the Realm of Icy Whispers

In the realm where shadows glide,
Icy whispers softly bide.
Twinkling stars in velvet skies,
Awakening the night's sweet sighs.

Silver leaves, a fragile sound,
Echoes in the frostbite ground.
Moments freeze, as time unwinds,
Secrets dance, the heart reminds.

Chilled breaths weave through the trees,
Carrying the winter's tease.
Each echo tells a tale confined,
In silence where our hopes aligned.

Yet amidst this frosted tint,
Quiet warmth begins to hint.
Within the cold, a spark ignites,
Guiding souls through icy nights.

Frosted Echoes in the Night

Frosted echoes cloak the ground,
Whispers hush, a soft surround.
Moonlight spills, a silver sheet,
Nature rests, the world's heartbeat.

Glistening threads, a woven dream,
In the dark, they dance and gleam.
Crisp air fills with stories old,
Held in the night, a tale retold.

Each silent step through winter's breath,
Carries warmth beyond sweet death.
Frozen whispers urge us near,
In this space, we shed our fear.

Cold embraces hold us tight,
In the tender arms of night.
Through the frost, our spirits glide,
In echoes where our hearts reside.

Ghosts of Crystalline Silence

Ghosts of silence drift and weave,
In the cold, they softly leave.
Crystals shimmer, lost in time,
Fractured light, a ghostly rhyme.

Through the stillness, shadows play,
Lingering where memories stray.
Glacial forms, a tale retold,
In the heart, a warmth of gold.

Each sigh of frost reveals the past,
Moments shared, forever cast.
In whispers deep, the spirits speak,
A language soft, yet bold and sleek.

Amidst the chill, our hopes arise,
Guided by the frozen skies.
In this silence, we ignite,
The strength to dream through winter's night.

Frosted Dreamscapes of White

In a world of snow so bright,
Whispers float in pure delight.
Each flake tells a silent tale,
Carving paths, a dreamlike trail.

Trees wear coats of gleaming white,
Beneath the moon's soft, silver light.
Crystals dance on winter's breath,
Nature's art, a quilt of death.

Children laugh, their joy runs deep,
Building forts, in snow they leap.
Snowmen stand with playful grace,
In this frosted, vast embrace.

Stars twinkle in a velvet sky,
As snowflakes tumble, drift, and fly.
A tranquil hush envelops all,
In this wonderland so small.

The sun will rise, the day will chime,
But winter's dreams are pure and prime.
As frost gives way to spring's warm touch,
In memories, we hold it much.

A Dance of Shimmering Flakes

Under the glow of fading light,
Frosted flakes begin their flight.
Twisting softly, they descend,
Nature's dance, a graceful blend.

Each flake spins a tale untold,
Of winter's magic, brave and bold.
They shimmer bright with every sway,
In a ballet, they gently play.

Whispers of frost fill the air,
As if the world holds gentle care.
A tapestry of white and blue,
Crafted by the chill so true.

The ground dons a blanket so fine,
While branches spark with silver twine.
The quiet hum of winter's breath,
In every flake, a spark of depth.

When winter's night begins to gleam,
In the stillness, we will dream.
A dance unfolds, a soft embrace,
In this shimmering, frosted space.

Glimmering Tapestry of Chill

Across the fields, the snowflakes fall,
A glimmering weave, enchant us all.
Threads of ice in twilight's glow,
Kissing the earth, a crystal show.

Whispers of winter chill the air,
Heartbeats echo in the flare.
Nature's art, so pure and still,
In every breath, we find the thrill.

A canvas painted, white and bright,
Beneath the stars, it shines at night.
With every gust, the treetops bow,
A moment cherished, here and now.

As dawn awakens, frost begins,
To melt away, yet still, it spins.
In our hearts, this chill will stay,
A glimmering memories' ballet.

The seasons change, yet whispers call,
Embracing winter's frosty thrall.
As time slips by, we softly sigh,
In this tapestry, we dream and fly.

Beneath the Frozen Canopy

Beneath the trees, so tall and grand,
A frozen world, a silver band.
Each branch adorned with icy lace,
A secret realm, a hidden space.

The forest hums with tales of old,
In whispers soft, the stories told.
The snowflakes dance, a sacred rite,
In the realm of winter's night.

Footprints trace the path of dreams,
Among the ferns and frozen beams.
Nature holds us in her sway,
In this chill, we find our play.

Stars peek through the frosty leave,
Their twinkle warms our heart, believe.
A canopy of dreams above,
Wrapped in winter's gentle love.

With every breath, the magic grows,
As deep within, the stillness flows.
Eternal whispers, snowflakes sigh,
Beneath this canopy, we fly.

An Ecru Canvas Enfolding

Upon the stretch of winter's breath,
A canvas soft, untouched by death.
Ecru dreams in silence flow,
Where whispers of the frosts bestow.

In gentle strokes, the shadows play,
A fleeting dance at end of day.
Nature's palette, pure and bright,
Transforms the world in muted light.

Footprints break the stillness deep,
As secrets of the snowflakes leap.
Each flake a story, pure, divine,
An artful tale etched in time.

The branches wear their silken tears,
Cradling winter's frozen years.
An ecru canvas, vast and wide,
Holds dreams where warmth and hope abide.

With every chill, the heartbeats blend,
In this serene, enchanted mend.
A tranquil hush, a world so grand,
On ecru tapestries we stand.

Lattice of Winter's Grace

Through icy webs, the sunlight peeks,
In lattice forms where nature speaks.
A woven tale of frost and light,
Under the spell of starry night.

Framed in silver, every branch,
A winter's work, a graceful dance.
Nature's jewels, like whispers tossed,
In the lattice, love embossed.

The air is crisp, the world aglow,
As echoes of the cold winds blow.
Each breath a cloud, a fleeting sigh,
In winter's grip, we learn to fly.

Beneath the skies, a quiet hush,
Life stirs beneath the gentle brush.
In lattice dreams, we find our place,
Embracing all, this winter's grace.

In every flake, a glimpse of art,
A tender touch that warms the heart.
We weave our hopes through icy lace,
In the embrace of winter's grace.

The Symphony of Chilled Hearts

In frozen realms where silence sings,
A symphony of chilled hearts brings.
The notes of winter, crisp and clear,
Awake the spirits, drawing near.

With every breath, the air we steal,
Melodies of frost, we feel.
A tranquil tune, the night unfolds,
As stories of the season are told.

In whispers of the icy breeze,
The world adorned with frozen trees.
Each falling flake, a gentle sound,
In this sweet symphony unbound.

As twilight wanes, the stars align,
With chilled hearts beating in design.
A chorus of the cold we share,
In the stillness, we find our prayer.

Together we shall stand in awe,
In winter's grip, without a flaw.
A symphony in white and blue,
Where chilled hearts find their love anew.

A Mosaic of Icy Bliss

A mosaic formed in shades of white,
Each patch a story, pure delight.
Glistening crystals, tough yet frail,
In nature's grasp, we set our sail.

Patterns glow in the morning sun,
Each icy piece a race we run.
With every gleam, a spark ignites,
In winter's world, we claim our sights.

Gentle layers, cold embrace,
Nature's quilt, a soft, sweet face.
As shadows dance on snow-clad ground,
In this mosaic, bliss is found.

Through winter storms, our spirits rise,
In every flake, a fleeting prize.
Together bound by icy bliss,
In the embrace, nothing amiss.

With laughter shared and memories bright,
We weave our tales in purest light.
A mosaic crafted, love's insist,
In every heartbeat, warmth persists.

The Ethereal Dance of Winter's Breath

Whispers of cold in the frosty night,
Dancing moonlight, casting silver bright.
Snowflakes twirl in a graceful leap,
Nature's embrace, in silence deep.

Pines stand tall, with snow-laden arms,
Guarding secrets, whispering charms.
The chill in the air, a gentle caress,
Wrapped in dreams, we find our rest.

Footsteps crunch on the glittering ground,
Each sound echoes, a delicate sound.
The world in white, a magical hue,
A canvas painted with sparkling dew.

Fires crackle in the hearth's warm hold,
Stories shared as the night grows cold.
Outside, the beauty of winter's grace,
Inside, the warmth of a cherished space.

A world transformed, calming the mind,
In winter's breath, peace we find.
The ethereal dance, serene and vast,
Moments like snowflakes, fleeting, yet last.

Crystalline Pathways of Serenity

In winter's realm, the pathways gleam,
Crystalline beauty, like a waking dream.
Each step forward, a soft, white trail,
Guided by stars, we shall not fail.

Branches adorned with frost's embrace,
Nature whispers in a tranquil space.
Silence lingers in the cool night air,
Magic unfolds, beyond compare.

The moon casts shadows, slender and long,
While gentle breezes hum a sweet song.
Every crystal reflects a light,
A dance of shadows in the night.

Time slows down in this winter's grace,
Harmony found in nature's face.
A world reborn, serene and bright,
The crystalline pathways, a heart's delight.

With every breath, serenity flows,
In winter's dance, our spirit knows.
A moment cherished, a treasure rare,
Crystalline pathways lead us there.

Echoes of the Frozen Horizon

Beyond the hills, where the wind does sigh,
Frozen horizons touch the endless sky.
Whispers of silence, a haunting tune,
Under the watchful eye of the moon.

Icicles hang from the eaves like tears,
Carved by the touch of lingering years.
Echoes of footsteps, soft and slow,
Marking the path where memories flow.

The landscape stretches, vast and wide,
Snow-covered valleys where dreams reside.
A fragile beauty in the icy glade,
A sanctuary where shadows fade.

Stars twinkle bright in the midnight blue,
Pointing the way for the wandering crew.
Each breath of winter, a story told,
Of frozen horizons, brave and bold.

In this stillness, the heart takes flight,
Chasing echoes, lost in the night.
The frozen world, a tranquil sea,
In its embrace, we long to be free.

Fragments of Brilliance in Winter

Shards of ice glimmer in the morning light,
Fragments of brilliance, a wondrous sight.
Each frosted surface, a story untold,
Whispering secrets of winter's hold.

The air is crisp, filled with magic's spark,
Footprints lead where the wild things hark.
A tapestry woven of white and blue,
Nature's artistry in every view.

Trees wear coats of glistening frost,
In this beauty, we count not the cost.
Moments captured, so fleeting and rare,
Fragments of brilliance dance in the air.

As twilight descends, colors collide,
The horizon blushes, winter's pride.
A fiery sunset in a frozen land,
Painting warmth with a delicate hand.

In winter's grasp, our spirits ignite,
Fragments of brilliance, pure delight.
A season of stillness, yet full of cheer,
In its embrace, we hold what is dear.

Gossamer White

In the hush of winter's night,
Snowflakes dance, a soft delight.
Whispers of frost on frozen trees,
Nature's art in gentle breeze.

Blankets cover earth below,
Silent secrets, pure and slow.
Moonlight glistens, soft and bright,
In the calm of gossamer white.

Footprints trace the quiet ground,
In stillness, beauty's found.
Every flake, a fleeting dream,
In this tranquil, silver beam.

Winter's breath, cool and clear,
Brings a sense of peace and cheer.
Gossamer threads in frosty air,
Sparkling gems, beyond compare.

As dawn breaks, colors bloom,
Painting life where shadows loom.
Yet the white remains, so rare,
A soft promise lingering there.

When the World Holds its Breath

Stillness wraps the waking day,
Time pauses, slips away.
In a moment, all is clear,
The universe, draws near.

Clouds gather, skies softly turn,
A hushed anticipation burns.
Nature waits, with bated breath,
A fragile line between life and death.

Birds cease their vibrant song,
To this peace, they too belong.
Everything seems to align,
In this sacred, quiet time.

The sun hangs low, a golden hue,
In this stillness, dreams come true.
Hearts beat softly, hopes arise,
In the silence, love never dies.

Moments stretch, a timeless dance,
Inviting all to take a chance.
When the world holds its breath,
Magic flows, defying death.

Fragile Geometries

Delicate lines, drawn in the air,
Symmetry whispers everywhere.
Shapes of nature, soft and bright,
   Crafting beauty in the light.

Petals open, angles traced,
In each bloom, a touch of grace.
Life's equation, simple yet grand,
Fragile geometries, hand in hand.

The spider weaves, a silken thread,
Patterns forming, beautifully spread.
Nature's designs, a wondrous sight,
   In the tapestry of day and night.

Waves on shores, a rhythmic dance,
   Curves and circles in a trance.
   Every form a whispered plea,
In fragile geometries, we see.

Stars above, in cosmic art,
Patterns echo, speak to the heart.
Mathematics of the soul's embrace,
   In every shape, a sacred space.

Nature's Crystal Ballet

In the forest, shadows play,
Leaves pirouette, night and day.
Moonlit beams on branches glide,
Nature's dancers, side by side.

Gentle winds, a soft refrain,
Rustling whispers, a sweet domain.
Every step, a graceful turn,
In this ballet, hearts will burn.

Rippling streams, a shimmering flow,
Reflecting light in a graceful show.
Pebbles leap, and waters swirl,
In the crystal dance of the world.

Birds take flight, a soaring leap,
In the sky, their echoes sweep.
Wings unfurl, in bright display,
Nature's rhythm, come what may.

As dawn awakes, the stage is set,
A wondrous cast we won't forget.
In every moment, pure delight,
Nature's ballet, shining bright.

Icebound Whispers in the Twilight

In the dusk where shadows play,
Whispers drift on icy air.
Frozen dreams of yesterday,
Dance beneath the moon's cold glare.

Stars are sprinkled overhead,
Like diamonds on a darkened sheet.
Silence wraps the world in tread,
The heart hears winter's heartbeat.

Frosted branches loom and bend,
Crispness bites the wandering mind.
Time seems lost, with no end,
In the stillness, peace we find.

Echoes of a world so bright,
Captured in this shimmering night.
Every breath a misty sigh,
Underneath the twilight sky.

Nature sleeps, but softly hums,
Songs that float like snowflakes high.
In these moments, silence comes,
Icebound whispers never die.

Veils of Frosted Ornaments

Glittering in morning's light,
Windows dressed in frosty lace.
Nature's gems, a pure delight,
Adorn the world with gentle grace.

Branches wear their icy gowns,
Each one a sparkling fairy tale.
In the stillness, beauty crowns,
The earth, a canvas to unveil.

Snowflakes twirl in wild ballet,
Graceful forms that kiss the ground.
Whispers of the cold convey,
A magic spell that can be found.

Frosted orbs, a tender sight,
Reflecting warmth of sun's embrace.
Veils enfold the day from night,
Hiding secrets in their space.

As daylight wanes, the glimmers fade,
But memories of beauty stay.
In night's hold, the dreams are made,
Veils of frost lead hearts away.

Spirals of Icy Whimsy

In a world of swirling white,
Spirals dance in frosty air.
Whimsy spins with pure delight,
Nature's art beyond compare.

Snowflakes fall like whispered dreams,
Twinkling in their fragile flight.
Each one caught in sunlight beams,
Creating magic, pure and bright.

Children laugh beneath the trees,
With snowballs flying, joy unleashed.
Merry chaos, hearts at ease,
In this moment, all's released.

Footprints trace a winding path,
Leading to adventures new.
In the chill, there's no wrath,
Just the warmth of friendship's view.

Spirals of joy in every flake,
Painting wonder on our souls.
In winter's grasp, we never break,
Unite as we dance and roll.

The Quiet Art of Winter's Touch

Gentle whispers in the frost,
Winter's brush, a soft caress.
Nature breathes, no warmth is lost,
In the chill, we find our rest.

Hushed the world beneath the snow,
Every sound a muffled sigh.
Silent, graceful, spirits flow,
In this peace, we learn to fly.

Ice crystals adorn each bough,
Laced with silver, pure and bright.
Nature's quiet, holy vow,
Cloaked in velvet, wrapped in night.

Time stands still, the air is clear,
A tranquil heart finds solace here.
In winter's grip, we shed our fear,
Embracing all that's held so dear.

The art of stillness, soft yet bold,
Reminds us that we're not alone.
In this beauty, life unfolds,
Winter's touch calls us back home.

Glistening Strings of Frosty Dreams

In the hush of night, soft whispers call,
Glistening stars in an embroidered shawl.
Each breath a mist, a frosty delight,
Dreams woven tight in the blanket of night.

Silvery shadows dance on frozen streams,
Casting tales of past in shimmering beams.
A world enchanted, wrapped in lace,
Overflowing with magic, a celestial embrace.

Through the trees, a gentle breeze weaves,
Lullabies sung by silvery leaves.
Nature's own symphony, a quiet scheme,
Unraveling gently the threads of the dream.

Footsteps leave prints in the crusty snow,
Guided by starlight, where wishes flow.
Each glimmer a promise, soft yet bright,
Binding the heart to the stillness of night.

Glistening stars, like pearls on the ground,
Keepers of secrets that whisper around.
In the silence, joy and wonder gleam,
Such is the beauty of frosty dreams.

A Symphony in White and Silver

Softly the world wraps in a blanket of white,
A symphony played in the still of night.
Silver notes twinkle, like stars on the wing,
Each flake a story, a joy to bring.

Crystals cascade from heavens above,
Melodies echo, as the earth falls in love.
Whirls of enchantment, a graceful dance,
Nature performs in a trance-like romance.

Footfalls are muffled, a hush in the air,
Whispers of winter are tender and rare.
The moon sheds its light, a silvery hue,
Painting the landscape in soft shades of blue.

Under the heavens, where dreams entwine,
A symphony's cadence, so gentle, divine.
Join in the rhythm of this wintry play,
Where white and silver forever stay.

As dawn approaches, the music will fade,
Yet echoes of beauty in hearts will cascade.
In quiet reflection, let your spirit soar,
For a symphony of winter lives evermore.

Moonlit Crystals and Whispering Winds

The moon casts its glow on a crystalline night,
Whispering winds weave tales filled with light.
Each snowflake dances, a delicate show,
Carried by breezes, where secrets flow.

Crystals glimmer beneath a silver sky,
Silent reflections of a world passing by.
Nature's soft sighs in the evening breeze,
Invite us to listen, to pause, and to seize.

Frozen horizons stretch far and wide,
With echoes of magic where dreams abide.
A canvas of wonder, painted in ice,
Inviting the heart to listen and entice.

Through the stillness, enchantments blend,
Moonlit paths where shadows bend.
Whispers of winter, soft as a prayer,
Entwine with the night, a tranquil affair.

In this sacred moment, let silence speak,
As moonlit crystals glow, gentle and meek.
Together we'll wander through wonder's embrace,
In the still of the night, we'll find our place.

Poetry of the Frosted Expanse

In the frosted expanse, a canvas so white,
Nature unfurls, a vision of light.
Each crystal a verse, uniquely sublime,
Composed by the chill, swept away by time.

Mountains of wonder, cloaked in the cold,
Hold stories of mystique, quietly told.
With each breath taken, the air crisp and clear,
Embrace the enchantment that winter draws near.

Footsteps crunch softly on the frozen ground,
Where echoes resound in the silence profound.
The artistry whispers in shadows and glow,
Of landscapes adorned in fresh sheets of snow.

Stars punctuate darkness, a heavenly quilt,
Wraps the world gently, where dreams are built.
In the poetry crafted by winter's own hand,
Each line a caress of the earth and the land.

So here in this moment, we gather and sigh,
Breathing in beauty that quietly flies.
In the heart of the frost, let our spirits dance,
To the rhythms of nature's serene expanse.

The Dance of Icy Petals

In the hush of wintry night,
Petals swirl in silver light.
Whispers through the gentle breeze,
Nature's art, a silent tease.

Frosty fingers trace the ground,
Softest snowflakes all around.
Like dancers twirling on their way,
In beauty's grip, they softly sway.

Beneath the moon's cold, watchful glow,
Icy blossoms start to grow.
A crystal waltz, they interlace,
In winter's heart, a tender grace.

With every turn, the shadows play,
In their world, we'll drift away.
Among the petals, pure and free,
Wrapped in dreams, just you and me.

So let us lose ourselves and flow,
In this dance, where cold winds blow.
The icy petals paint the night,
In their beauty, we find light.

Tapestry of Frost

A tapestry of silver threads,
Woven soft where daylight spreads.
Frosted leaves in sun's embrace,
Nature's art, a timeless grace.

Each inch gleams with crystal pride,
In this world, the chill won't hide.
Patterns etched on windows clear,
Winter's breath is finally near.

Mirrored pools reflect the sky,
Where clouds drift by, oh so high.
Beneath the frost, the earth whispers,
Secrets of the winter lusters.

With every spark, a story spun,
Of days gone by, of autumn's run.
In layers deep, the magic grows,
In frosty hues, the season glows.

So walk with me on this bright morn,
Through frosted paths where dreams are born.
In the tapestry, we find our tune,
A dance of frost beneath the moon.

Veils of Enchantment

Veils of mist, so soft and pale,
Whisper secrets on the trail.
Magic lingers in the air,
In every breath, a spell to share.

The forest sings in hushed delight,
Where shadows blend with morning light.
Each step brings a woven dream,
In nature's trance, we silently gleam.

A tapestry of whispered lore,
Among the trees, we long for more.
In every flicker, a memory,
Bound in mist, so wild and free.

Through veils of enchantment, we shall roam,
Finding realms we've never known.
Let the magic pull us near,
In this moment, all is clear.

Together in this mystic sight,
We dance beneath the fading light.
Wrapped in veils, we find our way,
In the shadows, night turns to day.

Lost in the Flurry

Snowflakes swirl in wild embrace,
A dance of white, a fleeting chase.
Lost in the flurry, hearts set free,
In winter's grip, just you and me.

As laughter echoes through the air,
Every moment, beyond compare.
A world transformed, so pure, so bright,
In a tapestry of shimmering white.

Let the chilly winds guide our feet,
In the snow, a rhythm sweet.
The flurry covers all we've known,
In its warmth, we find our home.

In the embrace of soft snowfall,
We surrender, we hear the call.
With each flake, memories arise,
Beneath the stormy, painted skies.

So dance with me through the night,
In laughter, in love, pure delight.
For in this flurry, we will stay,
Together, forever, come what may.

The Fragile Palette of Winter

Frosted whispers on the breeze,
Colors muted, soft as dreams.
Trees stand tall, bare branches sway,
In the hush of winter's day.

Silver glints on pristine snow,
Nature rests, prepares to grow.
Echoes dance in icy light,
A fleeting beauty, pure and bright.

Crystals hang like fragile glass,
Moments fleeting, yet they last.
Under skies of deepened gray,
Winter's hand will paint the way.

The world takes pause, a breath in time,
Silent echoes, soft as rhyme.
Chill descends in quiet grace,
Carving dreams in winter's space.

Each breath fogs the air anew,
Fleeting warmth in skies of blue.
A palette rich with shades of white,
In winter's hold, the world feels right.

Echoes of the Chill

Whispers drift upon the air,
Nature stirs with gentle care.
Footsteps crunch on frozen ground,
In the stillness, peace is found.

The sun dips low, a golden hue,
Shadows stretch, the day bids adieu.
Winter breathes on every face,
Time seems lost in this embrace.

Each flake falls with tender grace,
Filling up the quiet space.
Stars peek through the night's embrace,
Echoes linger, leave no trace.

Biting winds sing softly low,
Secrets buried in the snow.
Moments slip, then fade away,
Yet the chill will always stay.

Through the cold, warmth still remains,
Hearts ignite where hope sustains.
In every echo, soft and clear,
Winter whispers, we must hear.

Whispers of Winter's Veil

The world wrapped in silver white,
Softly glowing in the night.
Underneath the moon's soft gaze,
Winter dances, gently sways.

Frosty patterns on the pane,
Nature weaves her cool refrain.
Silent woods, a breath held tight,
Whispers echo through the night.

Shaking branches, laden low,
A soft promise wrapped in snow.
Time stands still in this ballet,
Beauty written in the gray.

Footsteps vanish, trails erased,
Hidden paths, a quiet grace.
In winter's heart, secrets dwell,
As we listen to the spell.

Harmonies of chill and light,
In the stillness, pure delight.
Winter's veil, a soft embrace,
Cradling dreams in frozen space.

Crystal Threads in the Silence

Glistening threads in morning's glow,
Nature's fabric, soft and slow.
Each detail a delicate art,
Winter's beauty, a tender heart.

Time is woven through the trees,
In the hush, a gentle breeze.
Crystal droplets, hanging low,
Harmonies of ebb and flow.

A blanket of white, pure and deep,
Legacies of dreams we keep.
Shadows dance in twilight's grace,
In the silence, find your place.

Beneath the surface, life awaits,
Hidden stories, open gates.
Each breath whispers, soft and clear,
Winter's truth we hold so dear.

Through the chill, we find our way,
In the night turning to day.
With crystal threads, we're intertwined,
In nature's arms, our hearts aligned.

Elysian Drift of Icebound Beauty

In the silence of the night,
Dreams drift softly, pure and bright.
Glistening whispers, a tranquil sight,
Veils of frost in silver light.

Frozen rivers, winds that sigh,
Beneath a vast, eternal sky.
Nature's canvas, stark yet nigh,
Beckons souls with gentle cry.

Each flake dances, a fleeting trace,
In this hallowed, frozen space.
Chasing shadows, time's embrace,
Life's pulse in winter's grace.

Branches wear a crystal crown,
A masterpiece of nature's gown.
Whispers echo, soft and brown,
In the hush, the world slows down.

Elysian dreams in chilly glow,
Where hopes and wishes softly flow.
In icebound beauty, spirits grow,
Transcending realms, we come to know.

Ethereal Frostwork on the Ground

Delicate patterns spread like lace,
On the earth, a frozen embrace.
Nature's brush leaves no trace,
Yet whispers softly in this place.

Ethereal shades, so vivid and bright,
Sparkle beneath the pale moonlight.
Each breath comes out, a cloud in flight,
In this wonder, pure delight.

Frost-kissed grasses shimmer and dance,
Inviting all to take a chance.
To wander here, in a frozen trance,
And greet the cold with a knowing glance.

Leaves adorned with icy thread,
Shimmering jewels where spirits tread.
With each step softly led,
We find the warmth where dreams are fed.

Ethereal frostwork, a fleeting show,
Nature's wonder, soft and slow.
In this world of frost and glow,
Magic awaits, let your heart flow.

Delicate Whirls of Frigid Light

Swirling dances in the air,
Delicate whirls, like whispered prayer.
Each shimmering flake, beyond compare,
A symphony of chill laid bare.

Frosted secrets, hidden in white,
Glowing softly with a hint of night.
Whispers echo, taking flight,
In the stillness, pure delight.

Cold stars twinkle in the sky,
As the moon watches, standing by.
In this world, we learn to fly,
With every breath, we reach up high.

In the frosty air, spirits gleam,
Carving paths in a frozen dream.
With each step, a gentle beam,
Nature's magic flows like cream.

Delicate whirls, a ballet bright,
Whispering tales through the night.
In this realm where hearts ignite,
Frigid light brings us to new height.

Enchanted Patterns in the Cold

Patterns whisper on the ground,
In the quiet, secrets found.
Enchanted trails where dreams abound,
In the cold, our hearts unbound.

A tapestry of snowflakes bright,
Spins a story under starlight.
Each had a journey, a silent flight,
In winter's grasp, a pure delight.

Winds waltz softly through the trees,
Telling tales upon the breeze.
Nature's brush paints as she sees,
Crafting magic with such ease.

Glittering pathways, winding grace,
Lead us to a sacred place.
Every step, a warm embrace,
With every heartbeat, time we chase.

Enchanted patterns, cold yet warm,
Whispering peace, a calming charm.
In winter's arms, we come to swarm,
Finding solace, safe from storm.

Mirage of Ice Under the Moonlight

Moonlight casts a silver hue,
Whispers ride the chilled night air.
Ice forms shapes, a fleeting view,
Frozen dreams beyond compare.

Crystal lakes, a silent gleam,
Stars twinkle in the frosty sky.
Mirage dances, like a dream,
Echoes fade, a soft goodbye.

Shadows lengthen, fading light,
Footsteps crunch on icy ground.
Nature quiet, pure delight,
Frozen whispers all around.

Refracted beams of pale white,
Glisten on the hands of time.
In the stillness, hearts take flight,
Lost in wonder, lost in rhyme.

In the night, where dreams take form,
A cold embrace, a sweet escape.
Mirage of ice, so soft, so warm,
In moonlit grace, our souls reshape.

Elegance Woven in Frosted Air

Winds weave tales through branches bare,
Frosted whispers, sweet and rare.
Silken threads in pale moon's glare,
Nature's art beyond compare.

Each breath lingers, crisp and bright,
Cascading snowflakes lace the night.
A dance begins in pure delight,
Elegance held in frozen light.

Beneath a cloak of soft white hue,
Dreams unfold in gentle sway.
Frosted patterns, old and new,
Charmed by winter's quiet play.

In the stillness, hearts all yearn,
For the beauty, ever near.
Frosted air, where spirits burn,
In elegant moments, we appear.

Whispers of warmth in icy threads,
Binding us with gentle care.
In every sigh, a song spreads,
Elegance woven in frosted air.

Dance of the Frostflower

In the glade, a frostflower blooms,
Petals glisten, kissed by frost.
Dancing lightly, dispelling gloom,
In beauty's breath, we're never lost.

Each flake twirls in a gentle sway,
Nature's dance, a graceful art.
Whispers call as night turns gray,
Listening close, it warms the heart.

Cold winds carry soft refrains,
A lullaby for winter's night.
Frostflower skirts in silver chains,
Glowing softly, pure delight.

In the moon's embrace, it shimmers bright,
A fleeting glimpse, eternity.
Captivating in pale moonlight,
Frostflower's dance, in harmony.

As dawn approaches, bids adieu,
Its beauty lasts, though seasons change.
In every heart, it leaves its hue,
The dance of frost, forever strange.

Dreaming in a Feather of Ice

In the silence of a frigid night,
Feathers drift on frosty air.
Dreams take shape in purest white,
Whispers cradle all our care.

Hearts alight with sparkling hope,
Each breath dances on the freeze.
In gentle sways, we learn to cope,
Sweet reflections, winter's ease.

A tapestry of frosty grace,
Woven deep in starlit skies.
In our warmth, we find our place,
Dreaming soft, as the world sighs.

Glowing embers hide within,
Nestled deep beneath a veil.
In this moment, we begin,
Feathered wishes, tell the tale.

So let us linger in this field,
Where ice-kissed dreams forever flow.
In each heartbeat, warmth is sealed,
In a feather of ice, we glow.

Shimmering Silence

In twilight's calm, the stars awake,
Soft whispers weave through the still lake.
Moonlight dances on the gentle waves,
While shadows cradle the secrets it saves.

The world holds breath, a fleeting pause,
As silence envelops without cause.
Each shimmering glint, a story untold,
In the hush of night, mysteries unfold.

Branches whisper in the gentle breeze,
Nature's lullaby brings hearts to ease.
Calmness wrapped in a silky thread,
Where dreams are born, and fears are shed.

Beneath the stars, we find our way,
Lost in thoughts that softly sway.
In shimmering silence, time stands still,
A tranquil moment, a sacred thrill.

Luna's glow guides each wandering soul,
Illuminating paths, making hearts whole.
In the night's embrace, we find our grace,
In shimmering silence, we find our place.

Threads of Frost

Morning breaks with a silver gleam,
Nature sparkles, a winter dream.
Threads of frost on the window pane,
Nature's artistry, a fleeting gain.

The grass wears crystals, a jeweled crown,
Each blade glistening, no hint of brown.
Sunrise kisses the icy morn,
Painting whispers where dreams are born.

Footprints left in the soft white snow,
Stories hidden where cold winds blow.
With each step, the world feels new,
Wrapped in silence, a tranquil hue.

Trees adorned with a frosty lace,
Embrace the chill, a gentle grace.
In the crisp air, our laughter swells,
Echoing warm where the frosty dwells.

Evening falls, the stars ignite,
While threads of frost adorn the night.
In the quiet, magic resides,
As the winter's beauty gently guides.

Glistening Hush

Night unfurls its velvet cloak,
In the stillness, soft words evoke.
Lights twinkle like fireflies' dance,
In the glistening hush, there's a chance.

Gentle sighs weave through the air,
Moments of peace, beyond compare.
Shadows play in a tender glow,
Secrets whispered, soft and slow.

The world outside softly fades away,
In this calm, we dream and sway.
A glimmering hush wraps us tight,
Guiding hearts through the night.

Time holds its breath, a sacred pause,
Curled in warmth, from dusk we draw.
In each heartbeat, the night breathes deep,
In glistening hush, we find our sleep.

Stars watch over, a silent cheer,
Embracing whispers, drawing near.
In the stillness, hope and light,
In the glistening hush, all feels right.

Ethereal Flurries

Softly falling, a dance of white,
Ethereal flurries grace the night.
Whispers of snow on the gentle ground,
Magic lingers, a spell profound.

Children laugh, their joy untold,
In winter's arms, the world feels bold.
Frosted dreams in a snowy play,
Captured moments that drift away.

Each flurry tells of a tale seraphic,
In soft embraces, our hearts are graphic.
Stars align in a swirling dance,
In ethereal flurries, we find romance.

The world transformed, a canvas bright,
Painting whispers in the moonlight.
As flakes converge in a splendid rush,
We savor the gift of winter's hush.

With every breath, the crisp air sings,
In nature's wonder, our spirit swings.
Together wrapped in winter's cheer,
In ethereal flurries, we hold dear.

Comets of Ice

In the sky, they blaze and fly,
Comets of ice, a fleeting sigh.
Trailing tails of shimmering light,
Whispers of magic in the night.

Glistening against a velvet hue,
Each a story old and new.
Falling stars that dare to dance,
In a short-lived cosmic romance.

Frozen dreams in a galactic race,
Chasing shadows, leaving a trace.
Their brilliance fades, but still we yearn,
For the night when they return.

Wishes carried on their flight,
Caught in wonder, pure delight.
Silent watchers of our fate,
Comets of ice, we celebrate.

In the darkness, they will gleam,
A tapestry of dreams extreme.
Light the sky with tales untold,
Comets of ice, both fierce and bold.

A Dream on the Wind

Soft whispers carried high,
A dream on the wind, it starts to fly.
Drifting through the endless blue,
It dances lightly, pure and true.

With each breeze, it twirls and sways,
A melody of forgotten days.
Caught in gales of hopeful sighs,
Its spirit soars through open skies.

With the sun, it plays a game,
Gentle shadows call its name.
Through fields and valleys, it will roam,
Finding solace far from home.

Echoes of laughter in tapestry spun,
A world of wonder, just begun.
On the wind, a wish takes flight,
Illuminating the heart's delight.

As night falls, stars appear to gleam,
Guiding the path of the dream.
Hold it close, don't let it fade,
A dream on the wind, unafraid.

The Quiet of Falling

In the twilight, silence creeps,
The quiet of falling, as the world sleeps.
Leaves drift softly, whispers shared,
Nature's hush, a moment bared.

Each flake of snow, a breath in the air,
Blanketing all with tender care.
Crystals swirl in a gentle glide,
The quiet of falling, our hearts abide.

Moonlight glimmers on frozen streams,
Cradling dreams in silver beams.
Time stands still in this embrace,
The calmness held, a sacred space.

In this stillness, we find our way,
Lost in shadows of the day.
Underneath the stars so bright,
The quiet of falling feels just right.

Let the world fade into night,
In this silence, hearts take flight.
Embrace the moment, soft and small,
In the quiet of falling, we find it all.

Silence in White

A canvas stretched, wide and bright,
Wrapped in layers of silence in white.
Gentle flakes dance from above,
Soft kisses from the skies we love.

Footprints mark the frosty ground,
In this hush, pure peace is found.
The world transforms in softest shade,
A timeless beauty, never fade.

Whispers echo through the pines,
Nature's art in graceful lines.
Each moment still, as if to say,
Silence in white leads the way.

Winter's breath, a soothing balm,
In this tranquil, icy calm.
Hearts wrapped warm, we feel the glow,
In silence, find the love we know.

As twilight drapes its velvet cloak,
The night unfolds, a tender spoke.
In every flake, a dream ignites,
In the silence of white, our spirit lights.

The Stillness of Cold

In the hush of winter's breath,
Whispers dance on frozen ground.
Each flake falls with gentle grace,
Echoes soft, a silent sound.

Trees adorned with coats of white,
Holding secrets of the night.
Time seems frozen in its place,
Nature's still, a quiet space.

The moon hangs low, a silver gem,
Softly lighting the frost's hem.
Footsteps crunch on icy trails,
Winter's peace, a calm prevails.

Breath, it swirls in misty clouds,
The world wrapped in velvet shrouds.
Flowing rivers sleep and wait,
In this stillness, I contemplate.

A lone owl calls from the trees,
Carried softly with the breeze.
In the quiet, hearts can heal,
In winter's arms, we find what's real.

Icicle Serenade

Hanging bright from eaves so high,
Icicles glisten, catch the eye.
Dripping softly, a quiet tune,
Singing secrets of the moon.

In the thaw of midday light,
Melodies of winter bright.
Nature's orchestra starts to play,
As the frost begins to sway.

Each drop falls, a crystal clear,
Carving paths, where warmth draws near.
Their dance is brief, yet oh so sweet,
A fleeting joy, a happy beat.

The sun shines down, warmth's embrace,
Wrapping the world in tender grace.
Icicle tears now start to flow,
A serenade, a winter show.

As night falls, the chill returns,
Under stars, the cold still yearns.
Yet in the dark, we find the light,
Icicles shine, glittering bright.

Beneath the Ice Stars

Underneath a blanket cold,
Frozen dreams and stories told.
Stars peep through the icy night,
Whispers wrapped in silver light.

The world is still, a world of white,
Where shadows blend with the night.
Breath of winter, crisp and clear,
Nature rests, yet draws us near.

Fishing lines on frozen lakes,
Silent moments, quiet shakes.
Reflections dance in icy pools,
Where the heart knows winter's rules.

The sky above, a canvas deep,
Dreams are sewn where the night creeps.
Beneath the ice, as stars implore,
Life awaits, forevermore.

And as dawn breaks, shadows fade,
A gentle warmth, the light cascades.
Beneath the ice, the pulse remains,
In the heart, winter's refrains.

Veils of Flake and Light

Snowflakes fall in soft descent,
Veils of white, a gift well-meant.
Each one unique, a fleeting kiss,
In their dance, we find our bliss.

Beneath the boughs, the world transformed,
In their magic, hearts warmed.
Twilight glows, the colors blend,
As day to night begins to bend.

Frozen streams in quiet glades,
Casting shadows, soft cascades.
In the hush, our spirits soar,
Finding peace, forevermore.

Frosted whispers brush the trees,
Carrying tales upon the breeze.
Veils of light in winter's grasp,
Moments cherished, dreams held fast.

As night descends, starlit skies,
A tapestry where silence lies.
We walk the paths where snowflakes fall,
In winter's grace, we feel it all.

Portrait of a Frostbitten Dawn

The sun whispers soft and pale,
Casting shadows, a fragile veil.
Ice crystals cling to barren trees,
Nature's breath hangs in the breeze.

Colors bleed into the light,
Ghostly hues of winter's night.
Each moment holds a frozen frame,
A world transformed, never the same.

Silence reigns in the crisp air,
Every heartbeat a tender prayer.
Frosted whispers weave and twine,
In the dawn where shadows dine.

The stillness sways with unseen grace,
As time merges, leaves no trace.
In the chill, a fire ignites,
A tender warmth in frosty bites.

Awake, the world unfolds anew,
A portrait painted deep and true.
In each breath of icy dawn,
A story told, an echo drawn.

Celestial Threads in a Frozen Meadow

Stars descend in diamond dust,
Twirling softly, a cosmic gust.
Over meadows, soft and wide,
Where shadows and frost abide.

A tapestry of silver lace,
Twinkling in the night's embrace.
Frozen whispers weave the ground,
In silence, beauty is found.

Each grain of frost, a shining bead,
In the quiet, a gentle creed.
Nature's threads entwined so fine,
In the whispers of divine.

Serenity blooms where cold winds play,
In hues of winter, night and day.
Celestial dreams flutter and soar,
In meadows, untouched, forevermore.

The moon bathes all in silver light,
Casting echoes of beauty bright.
Under the stars, hearts align,
In the frozen meadow, divine.

The Lace of Winter's Heart

Snowflakes drift like delicate sighs,
In the hush of winter's eyes.
A tender lace, soft and white,
Weaving dreams into the night.

Each flake a whisper of what will be,
Carried gently on the breeze.
In their descent they dance and twirl,
Cradling the world in a frosted whirl.

Branches bow with a crystalline crown,
Beneath the weight of this soft gown.
Nature's heart beats slow and sweet,
In the embrace of winter's greet.

Silhouettes in white, a frozen scene,
Where the world wears a silken sheen.
Beneath the wonder, life stays still,
In winter's heart, a tranquil thrill.

In the silence, beauty sings,
As winter weaves its fragile strings.
In lace and frost, the quiet art,
A masterpiece, the winter's heart.

Elysium Beneath the Frost

Below the frost, a world awake,
In silence deep, for beauty's sake.
Roots entwined in layers of dreams,
Whispers held in icy streams.

Elysium waits, a secret space,
Hiding life in winter's grace.
Beneath the chill, warmth thrives unseen,
In the heart of where life's been.

Gentle hearts beat in the cold,
Stories of resilience told.
In the dark, soft pulses stir,
In every breath, a muted blur.

Nature rests, yet never ceases,
In the frost, her spirit pleases.
With every layer, life still grows,
In the hush, a mystery flows.

Though winter's grasp is strong and tight,
Hope dances in the fleeting light.
In Elysium beneath the frost,
Life's chorus sings, never lost.

Fantasia in the Blinding White

Snowflakes dance in the soft, cold air,
Illusions weave with a touch so rare.
A world transformed, pure, and bright,
Amidst the stillness, a wondrous sight.

Glistening crystals on branches sway,
Nature's breath in the light of day.
Every shadow tells a tale,
In this magic, we prevail.

Footsteps crunch on the frosty ground,
Echoes of joy in silence found.
Children laugh as they spin and glide,
In this fantasy, we all abide.

The hush of night brings a gentle hush,
Winter's coat in a dazzling rush.
Under the stars that softly gleam,
We wander deep into a dream.

In the whiteness, colors unfold,
Stories of warmth amidst the cold.
Endless wonders our hearts ignite,
In the blinding joy of pure delight.

Layers of Elegance and Chill

Frosted petals on a winter morn,
Whispers of beauty in silence born.
Each layer wrapped in crystal's hold,
Elegance graces the chilly bold.

Coats of white on the trees adorn,
Nature's palette early drawn.
Hints of blue in the fading light,
Serenade of dusk, a gentle flight.

Breath of the earth in the frosty air,
A tapestry woven with utmost care.
With every glance, new stories to tell,
In layers of wonder, we dwell.

Icicles hang like jewels at play,
Catching the sun in a bright display.
Chill of the breeze, a lover's sigh,
Ribbons of elegance swirling by.

Winter's embrace holds a secret grace,
In every corner, in every space.
Layer by layer, life's canvas reveals,
The art of chill, the heart it heals.

Veiled in Crystal and Moonlight

Under the veil of a silver night,
Whispers of magic shimmer and light.
In every corner, shadows gleam,
Nature wrapped in a dreamer's theme.

Moonlight dances on the frozen lake,
A serene vision, no heart could break.
Crystals rise from the earth's soft breath,
In stillness, they weave the thread of death.

Branches tangled in luminous lace,
Gracefully held in the night's embrace.
The world transforms, a mystical sight,
Veiled in the crystal of soft moonlight.

Echoes of silence serenade the dark,
Guided by the moon's gentle spark.
Every moment, ethereal and bright,
Lost in the magic of this delight.

Frosted dreams in the chill of night,
Speak of wonders that feel so right.
In this realm where secrets take flight,
Life shines anew in the soft moonlight.

Whispered Secrets of Ice and Cold

In the stillness, secrets unfold,
Whispers carried through the icy cold.
Nature speaks in a hushed refrain,
A language softly kissed by pain.

Frozen rivers, a tale of wait,
Captured dreams beneath the gate.
Each breath of chill, a story shared,
In the quiet, no heart is spared.

Crystalline structures rise and sway,
Echoing thoughts that linger and play.
Each fragile shard tells of the past,
Whispered secrets meant to last.

Snowflakes twirl in a ballet fine,
Tracing patterns by nature's design.
Every flake holds a moment dear,
In silence, we listen, we hear.

Empires built from the frost and dew,
Memories hidden, yet shining through.
In a world where ice and dreams behold,
Whispered secrets of ice and cold.

The Fabric of Frost

In twilight's breath, a shimmer glows,
Lace of frost on fallen leaves,
Nature's quilt, where silence flows,
Underneath the winter eaves.

Each crystal thread, a story spun,
Whispers soft of nights gone by,
A tapestry of shadows run,
Beneath the vast and starry sky.

The world transformed, a silver hue,
With every touch, a twinkling light,
In this realm, the old feels new,
As day gives way to peaceful night.

Footsteps crunch on icy trails,
A dance where all is still and bright,
Through frosted air, the wonder sails,
Embracing all in pure delight.

As dawn awakes, the sun ascends,
The fabric fades, but dreams remain,
In hearts, the magic never ends,
Where winter's chill births warmth again.

Hidden Jewels of Winter

Amidst the frost, the gems do gleam,
Each flake a treasure, soft and rare,
In quiet woods, a whispered dream,
Nature's bounty, rich and fair.

Underneath the snow's embrace,
A world adorned with icy lace,
Hidden jewels in frosty grace,
Await the kiss of spring's soft trace.

The frozen stream, a mirror wide,
Reflects the stars, a cosmic dance,
While winds of cold in shadows bide,
Each flurry tells a tale, a chance.

In quiet moments, take a breath,
As twilight falls, the night appears,
With every glance, a hint of death,
And life renewed through icy tears.

So cherish now the winter's glow,
For hidden gems are always near,
In this cold, a fire does flow,
A warmth within, a flicker clear.

Frost-Kissed Echoes

Echoes ring through frosty air,
Whispers soft from ages past,
Every breath a fleeting prayer,
In winter's grasp, our shadows cast.

The chill wraps close like a warm embrace,
Holding secrets between each breath,
With every step, the snow's soft face,
A memory shared with the quiet depth.

Footprints lead to thoughts unknown,
Where time stands still, and silence sings,
In snowy hush, we find our own,
Lost in moments that winter brings.

Beneath the stars, the frost does gleam,
In the stillness, the world awakens,
A dance of dreams begins to stream,
In every heart, a will unshaken.

So heed the echoes, let them flow,
Through icy paths, a journey shared,
For in the frost, we come to know,
The warmth of love, forever spared.

Whispering White

Amidst the hush, a whisper comes,
In blankets white, the earth does sleep,
A silent song in winter hums,
In shadows deep, the secrets keep.

Each flake that falls, a tale to tell,
Spun from dreams of frost and night,
In gentle waves, the breezes swell,
To wrap the world in purest light.

Under moonlight, the landscape glows,
With every curve, a fleeting grace,
As nature sighs, the magic flows,
Transforming all with soft embrace.

So let us wander through the pale,
Where softest whispers call us near,
In winter's grasp, our spirits sail,
To find the warmth that draws us here.

For in the white, we find our way,
Through murmurings of the cold,
In every dusk, in every day,
Whispering tales of love untold.

Nature's Lace

In the morning light, dew drops gleam,
A tapestry woven with nature's dream.
Leaves whisper secrets, soft and low,
As petals dance in the gentle flow.

Mountain peaks dressed in shimmering white,
Sunrise paints the sky, a beautiful sight.
Gentle breezes sing through the trees,
Nature's lace sways with perfect ease.

Rivers run clear, reflecting the sky,
With crystals of foam, they rush and sigh.
Birds flit and flutter on wings of grace,
In a world adorned by nature's lace.

Fields of wildflowers stretch and bloom,
A canvas alive, dispelling gloom.
Colors burst forth, a vibrant race,
In the warm embrace of nature's grace.

Evening descends, a soft lullaby,
Stars begin twinkling in the vast sky.
The moon whispers softly, an ethereal trace,
In the night's blanket, nature's lace.

Ephemeral Chill

A breath of ice, the world stands still,
Whispers of winter, an ephemeral chill.
Snowflakes descend, soft as a sigh,
Covering earth, where dreams lie high.

Skies turn gray, with clouds of lace,
Frost bites gently, a cold embrace.
Footprints crunch on a snowy road,
While silence deepens, a heavy load.

Trees wear coats of glistening frost,
In this stillness, warmth feels lost.
Yet in the hush, a beauty rare,
Each frozen breath hangs in the air.

Candles flicker against the night,
Shadows dance in the firelight.
Inside our hearts, embers will stay,
While outside, snow begins to play.

Tomorrow may bring the sun's warm thrill,
For now, we savor this ephemeral chill.
Wrapped in blankets, our minds will drift,
In winter's hold, we find our gift.

Frosted Wishes

In the quiet dawn, the world awakes,
Nature adorned, with frosted flakes.
Each breath is visible, a dreamy mist,
Carrying wishes that none could resist.

Children laugh in a glittering play,
Building snowmen throughout the day.
Frosted wishes float in the air,
In every twinkle, a joyful care.

The trees stand tall, cloaked in white,
Branches glisten in the soft twilight.
With every crunch beneath our feet,
Frosted wishes, a winter treat.

As night descends, stars gleam bright,
Frost paints shadows, soft and light.
With every wish whispered on the breeze,
Winter wraps us, with graceful ease.

Tomorrow brings what we hope and yearn,
Yet for now, let frosted wishes burn.
In this moment, joy feels near,
Wrapped in magic, winter's cheer.

Shards of Winter's Embrace

Icicles dangle, sharp and clear,
Shards of winter, crystal sheer.
The wind howls softly, a haunting song,
As nature whispers where we belong.

With every breath, the cold bites deep,
Secrets of frost in the silence seep.
Footsteps echo on the frozen ground,
In the stillness, magic is found.

The twilight casts a pale glow,
Snowflakes swirl in a graceful flow.
Each moment fleeting, like the light,
Shards of winter fade into night.

Warmth of a fire, a comforting sight,
Fingers curl around mugs, holding tight.
In the hearth's embrace, stories arise,
As shadows flicker, the heart complies.

For with every shard, a memory forms,
In winter's embrace, amidst the storms.
A season of beauty, challenge, and grace,
In the dance of the cold, we find our place.

Picturesque Brilliance of the Cold

Snowflakes dance on frosty air,
Sparkling diamonds everywhere.
Nature's canvas, white and bright,
Winter's beauty, pure delight.

Trees adorned with glistening frost,
Whispers of warmth, gently lost.
Crisp and clear, the world anew,
In this chill, our spirits grew.

Sunrise paints the horizon gold,
Shadows stretch, a tale unfolds.
Each moment, a frozen embrace,
Time slows down in this quiet place.

Footsteps crunch on the snow below,
Echoes of laughter, soft and low.
Happiness wrapped in winter's shroud,
Nature sings, both soft and loud.

As night falls, stars begin to blink,
In the stillness, we pause to think.
Picturesque brilliance, pure and bold,
Forever cherished, memories told.

Threads of Ice in the Morning Fog

Morning dawns, a muted hue,
Mist hovers like a gentle veil.
Threads of ice as sunlight breaks,
Nature's hush, a whispered tale.

Frozen grasses, sparkling bright,
Each droplet holds a secret tight.
Foggy whispers, landscapes unfold,
The magic of winter, bold yet cold.

Shadows flicker, trees stand bare,
Silhouettes against the misty air.
Threads of ice weave stories shy,
In this morning, spirits fly.

A silence deep, the world in sway,
As nature stirs to greet the day.
Softly glowing, with every breath,
Life awakens from winter's death.

In the distance, echoes call,
Blurring lines, a blanket falls.
Threads of ice, morning's glow,
A fleeting beauty, soft and slow.

Wandering through a Crystal Labyrinth

Wander lost in a frozen maze,
Crystal walls that gleam and blaze.
Each turn a wonder, each path a dream,
Nature's artistry, a shimmering theme.

Icicles hang like chandeliers,
Catching whispers, dreams, and fears.
Mirrors of frost reflect the soul,
In this labyrinth, we lose control.

Cold air bites, but hearts feel warm,
Embracing magic in every form.
Footprints lead, but twists abound,
In this realm, enchantment's found.

Every corner, a surprise waits,
Nature's beauty, it captivates.
Wandering here, time drifts away,
In crystal light, we long to stay.

As dusk descends, colors bleed,
Reflections dance on every bead.
Wandering still, the heart takes flight,
Through the labyrinth, into night.

The Gentle Caress of Frozen Twilight

Twilight falls on winter's breath,
A gentle caress, life and death.
Colors blend, the world at peace,
In frozen moments, we find release.

Soft whispers from the fading light,
Embrace the chill, a tranquil night.
Blue hues wrap around the trees,
An ode to stillness in winter's freeze.

Stars awaken, one by one,
Painting dreams when day is done.
Frozen dew on a silken thread,
Nature's quilt, a world well-read.

Time suspends in soft embrace,
As twilight casts its silver lace.
Every breath, a cloud of mist,
In this stillness, magic kissed.

The night deepens, shadows play,
In frozen twilight, we find our way.
The gentle caress, winter's art,
A quiet moment to warm the heart.

The Beauty Beneath

Beneath the surface, shadows play,
Colors hidden, yet bright and gay.
Whispers linger in the deep,
Secrets held, they rarely sleep.

In waters clear, reflections wane,
A world resides, yet feels no pain.
Dancing sunlight, gentle grace,
Nature's canvas, a warm embrace.

From riverbeds to ocean floors,
Life emerges, softly explores.
Each creature sings a silent tune,
In the depths, beneath the moon.

Hues of coral, shades of blue,
Every glance reveals something new.
Underneath the waves, they thrive,
In this realm, all feels alive.

So dive down deep, take a hold,
Find the stories long untold.
For in the depths, beauty remains,
A treasure chest of life's refrains.

Echoes in the Ice

In silence deep, the echoes call,
Through frozen realms, they rise and fall.
Crystals gleam beneath the frost,
Whispers of the cold are lost.

Footsteps crunch on hardened ground,
In every sound, a truth is found.
Nature's breath, it whispers low,
As time drifts by, soft and slow.

Branches heavy with coats of white,
Hold the memories of the night.
Each flake falls, a story spun,
Under the gaze of the waning sun.

In icy halls, reflections glide,
The beauty found in each divide.
A world asleep, yet deeply alive,
In this stillness, we learn to thrive.

So listen close to the frozen sighs,
Embrace the chill as daylight dies.
For in the heart of winter's breath,
Lies the echo of life and death.

Patterns of Silence

In the woods, a hush prevails,
Nature's pulse in soft exhale.
Leaves whisper tales of ancient time,
In patterns carved, both deep and prime.

Beneath the boughs, shadows blend,
Silent stories they intend.
Mossy carpets, soft and green,
Cover secrets yet unseen.

Rustling winds, they softly sigh,
In stillness, the heart learns to fly.
Every moment, a dance so sweet,
Where echoes of silence find their beat.

Footprints left upon the trail,
Each a mark in life's grand scale.
In the quiet, meanings form,
A refuge found within the storm.

So let the silence wrap you tight,
In its embrace, discover light.
For within the calm, we understand,
The patterns of life, forever planned.

A Tangle of Frost

Frosted branches twist and weave,
A tapestry that chills, yet leaves.
Nature's hands, with delicate art,
Wrap the world in a glistening heart.

In morning light, the crystals shine,
Each glimmer sparkles, a pure design.
Tangled twirls of icy white,
Dance in the dawn, a stunning sight.

Frozen pathways invite the brave,
Explore the paths that shadows pave.
Every turn reveals a dream,
In this wonderland, we gleam.

As the sun begins to rise,
Frost melts in a soft reprise.
Yet in the moment, beauty stays,
Captured in the frosty haze.

So walk through this enchanted maze,
In the chill of winter's gaze.
For within the tangle, there's a grace,
That time cannot erase.

Chill's Embrace

In the quiet of the night,
Whispers float on frosty air,
Moonlight glimmers, pure and bright,
Wrapped in cold, without a care.

Snowflakes dance on silver beams,
Cloaked in white, the world does sleep,
Dreams weave softly into dreams,
In the calm, our hearts do leap.

Each breath visible, a fleeting sigh,
Nature hushes, all is still,
Beneath the vast and starry sky,
Time slows down, bending to will.

Winter whispers in my ear,
Stories of the frozen land,
With each chill, I draw you near,
Together here, we stand hand in hand.

Gentle Glitter

Stars above, a gentle glow,
Twinkling softly in the night,
Winter's kiss, a melting snow,
Every flake, a pure delight.

Frozen branches, glistening bright,
Catching dreams of sparkling gold,
Silhouettes in the pale moonlight,
As the night becomes more bold.

A blanket white on fields afar,
Crystals sparkle, oh so fair,
Each moment bright as a shooting star,
Carried softly on the air.

Echoes of laughter, pure and clear,
Through the cold, they resonate,
In this magic, I hold dear,
Cherishing love, never late.

Frost-kissed Murmurs of the Night

Underneath the icy gaze,
Night unfolds its velvet cloak,
Winds do hum in whispered praise,
As the frost begins to soak.

Within the shadows, secrets hide,
Carried forth by chilling breeze,
Embraced by winter's quiet side,
Gently swaying ancient trees.

Every step, a crackling sound,
Echoes soft as dreams take flight,
Magic lingers all around,
In the frost-kissed, tranquil night.

Moments shared in whispered tones,
Beneath the stars, our hearts awake,
Amidst the frost, no one alone,
For in this peace, love's bonds we make.

Lacy Patterns on a Frozen Canvas

Delicate lace on winter's breath,
Patterns wrought in crystal sheen,
Nature paints with silent depth,
On a canvas pure and clean.

Silhouettes of trees adorn,
Each branch dressed in icy chains,
With every sunrise, beauty is born,
In this realm where silence reigns.

Footprints mark the snow so white,
Stories of where we have been,
In the glow of morning light,
Every moment, a precious glean.

Waltzing shadows, flickering flames,
Gathered close, we warm the night,
With laughter sweet and tender names,
Creating close our hearts' delight.

Shadows of Winter's Breath

The forest whispers in the dark,
Shadows dance 'neath silver skies,
Winter's hold leaves a stark mark,
As magic twinkles in our eyes.

Ghostly forms in moon's embrace,
Breathe in deeply, feel the chill,
Nature holds a solemn grace,
In every hush, the world stands still.

Branches sway with gentle ease,
Cradling dreams in frosty air,
Time is woven like the breeze,
In this quiet, nothing compares.

Each heartbeat echoes winter's song,
As the night unfolds its charm,
Together here, we both belong,
Safe within the winter's arm.